THE AUDACITY OF STUPID
FROM ABIGAIL TO JEZEBEL,
NAVIGATING TOXIC RELATIONSHIPS

CARLA HENRY-LEWIS

CONTENTS

Acknowledgments   vi

Introduction   1

Part I
BIBLICAL BLUEPRINTS FOR STUPIDITY

1. The Tale of Two Wives   7
2. The Tale of Two Husbands   13
3. Delilah & Samson   19
4. David & Bathsheba   25

Part II
MODERN STUPIDITY

5. The Tale of Tanisha and Tyrone   33
6. Keisha and the Church of What's Convenient   38
7. Political Stupid   44
8. Love Is Not Supposed to Hurt...Repeatedly   50

Part III
THE STUPIDITY SPECTRUM

9. The Signs You're Dating Stupid (Or Being Stupid)   59
10. The Justification Olympics   64
11. When Your Inner Child Loves a Clown   70
12. Co-Starring in Their Circus   75

Part IV
FREEDOM FROM FOOLISHNESS

13. Recovering From Stupid   83
14. Protecting Your Peace Like It's Beyoncé Tickets   88
15. Writing a New Story   93

Conclusion   98

Don't Let Your Wisdom Go to Waste 101

BONUSES
The Audacity of Stupid 105
🪨 The Stupidity Scorecard 110

*To my parents, **Dr. Lloyd Henry** and **Carolyn Winfrey Henry**, and to my siblings, **LaVerne, Carmen, Letitia, and Lloyd**— thank you for surviving my particular brand of stupidity.*

Whether we've been unconventional... or perfectly conventional (depending on who you ask), our lives have been stitched together with laughter, lessons, and a few well-timed side-eyes.

*We've learned—sometimes the hard way—that our gifts can be both a **blessing and a curse**, but we keep showing up, keep growing, and keep laughing (text thread is lit) anyway.*

I love you to the moon and back.

ACKNOWLEDGMENTS

This book is dedicated to every woman who's ever played the fool, stayed too long, or doubted her intuition—but woke up one day and chose peace over potential.

But before I learned how to spot foolishness in relationships, I learned how to **observe it in real time**—in meetings, in ministries, and in moments where power tried to silence purpose.

To my father, **Dr. Lloyd Henry**—thank you.

You were my first example of what it looks like to stand firm in the face of nonsense.

I watched you navigate church board meetings, school board standoffs, and hospital leadership rooms with **unshakable conviction**.

You didn't bow to titles. You didn't flinch when power postured.

You called out foolishness wherever it tried to hide—whether in a church, a corner office, or behind a "charming smile".

You were humble, but not silent.

You didn't seek favor—you demanded fairness.

And you taught me that peace doesn't mean passivity.

To my mother, **Carolyn Winfrey Henry**—thank you.

You, too, faced foolishness—but you believed in transformation.

As a lifelong educator, you walked into every classroom with the belief that **everyone could learn.**

And some did. But others?

They took advantage of your kindness.

They turned on you when it no longer served them.

And yet, you never lost your heart.

You are courage wrapped in compassion.

You are the lion who loved fiercely—and still does.

You taught me that strength isn't just in volume—it's in resilience.

This book was born out of **what I saw**, long before I could name it.

Out of boardrooms where egos clashed and bullies flexed.

Out of classrooms where grace was extended and sometimes returned with betrayal.

Out of the sacred space between wisdom and discernment.

So if I wrote boldly... it's because I was raised by people who **faced foolishness with integrity**.

Who fought for justice without needing applause.

Who showed me what it means to endure, to resist, to walk away when necessary—and to still walk in love.

Thank you for giving me both fire and finesse.

INTRODUCTION

"STUPID IS IN THE EAR OF THE HEARER"

"There is no greater illusion than the one we willingly believe because it soothes our ego or strokes our fear."

— ANONYMOUS, BUT IT COULD'VE BEEN YOUR
BEST FRIEND AFTER YOUR THIRD FAILED
SITUATIONSHIP

! **WARNING**: This book contains high levels of truth, side-eye, gospel shade, and holy sarcasm. If you're allergic to accountability, triggered by wisdom, or prone to defending the very nonsense that's stressing you out... you might want to read this with snacks, a journal, and a therapist on standby. You've been warned—with love. 🖋️

Let's get one thing straight from the jump: *this book is not about calling people stupid*. Well... not entirely. It's about the choices we make, the red flags we ignore, and the gut feelings we silence—all in the name of love, loyalty, politics, or plain ol' desperation. It's about the *audacity* of stupid: that bold, shameless confidence we sometimes have when we're doing something that makes no sense... but feels good for five minutes.

You've seen it. You've done it. So have I.

This isn't about shame. This is about *clarity*.

Some of the worst decisions we've ever made were wrapped in hope, seasoned with optimism, and deep-fried in dysfunction. We stayed too long. Voted too wrong. Believed too hard. And when it all blew up? We acted surprised, as if the warning signs hadn't been printed in neon and delivered by God's own FedEx.

But here's the kicker: we don't just make these choices in love—we make them in life. At the ballot box. In the breakroom. At the altar. On the group chat. Sometimes we're not just surrounded by stupid—we're sipping sweet tea with it on the porch, calling it "destiny."

This book is a love letter and a warning. A mirror and a magnifying glass. We'll revisit ancient biblical relationships that scream "Girl, run!" and modern-day messes that remind us: wisdom is a choice, and so is foolishness.

Through the stories of Abigail and Jezebel, Adam and Job, Samson and Delilah—and their present-day counterparts—you'll find patterns, parables, and plenty of "oh no she didn't" moments. Some will make you laugh. Others may sting. But every story is here to remind you: **you have options.**

We'll also explore why we indulge stupidity:

- Because we want to be Acknowledged.

- Because we crave Respect.

- Because we long to be Known.

Enter: **The A.R.K. Method**—a framework I developed to decode the real emotional drivers behind the conflicts we tolerate and the chaos we invite. Anger, Resentment, and Keen disappointment don't come from nowhere. They come from not being seen, heard, or understood. And if you don't deal with those unmet needs, you'll keep signing contracts with fools.

You'll also notice that this book isn't just about romantic stupidity. No ma'am. This is a multi-purpose, equal opportunity truth bomb. We'll tackle political foolishness, spiritual gaslighting, family drama, and workplace buffoonery. Because stupid wears many disguises—and some of them show up in pearls, prayer cloths, or press conferences.

And just in case you're wondering if this is too harsh... let me say it plain:

I'm not here to play nice with your delusion. I'm here to help you get free.

So, if you've ever said:

- "He ain't that bad once you get to know him."

- "Maybe they'll change if I just love them harder."

- "I can fix this—it's just a phase."

- "It's not that serious."

- "This is just how love works, right?"

Then honey... pull up a chair.

It's time to call a fool a fool, reclaim your peace, and laugh your way into wisdom. You don't have to keep participating in your own heartbreak. There's another way. There's a better choice. And no, you don't have to wait on permission to choose it.

Welcome to *The Audacity of Stupid*.

Let's get into it.

PART I
BIBLICAL BLUEPRINTS FOR STUPIDITY

1

THE TALE OF TWO WIVES

ABIGAIL VS. JEZEBEL

"When dealing with a fool, there are only two options: walk away or risk becoming one."

— *PROVERBIAL AUNTIE WISDOM, PASSED DOWN THROUGH SABBATH DINNER SIDE-EYES*

MEET THE WIVES: WISDOM VS. WICKEDNESS

There are two types of wives in the Bible who show us how to deal with foolish men—and they couldn't be more different.

On one side, we have **Abigail**—a woman married to a rich fool named Nabal, whose name literally meant *"fool."* Sis was beauty, brains, and backbone. The kind of woman who could command a room without raising her voice. She didn't wait for a miracle—she became the strategy.

On the other side, we have **Jezebel**—the ride-or-die for dysfunction. Power-hungry, cunning, and fully committed to her husband's mess like it was a ministry. She didn't just tolerate stupidity—she fertilized it and let it grow into full-blown evil.

Both women were married to men who couldn't lead wisely. But one chose diplomacy and discernment. The other chose domination and destruction.

Let's break down their stories—and more importantly, the choices they made.

ABIGAIL: THE QUEEN OF CRISIS MANAGEMENT

Abigail's husband, Nabal, had one job: don't embarrass the family. But of course, he did exactly that. David—yes, future King David—had protected Nabal's men in the fields, and all he asked in return was a little hospitality. A thank-you basket. A Chick-fil-A tray. Something.

But Nabal? He popped off. Disrespected David like he was just another shepherd in the streets. No gratitude. No honor. Just big "who dis?" energy.

David was ready to retaliate—sword drawn, ego bruised, ready to wipe out Nabal and every male in his house. And where was Nabal? Probably passed out drunk in a robe with his sandals on backwards.

Enter Abigail.

Without her husband's permission, she packed up supplies, met David on the road, and offered a peace offering with a side of humble pie. She acknowledged David's role, respected his power, and wisely appealed to his destiny—not his anger.

She didn't just save her household. She saved David from making a foolish, impulsive decision. And she did it with grace, humility, and high emotional intelligence.

By the time David got to Nabal, the man had dropped dead—likely from shock after realizing his wife was better at being a man than he was.

And what did David do next? He **married her.**

That's how you go from "wife of a fool" to "Queen in Waiting."

JEZEBEL: THE PATRON SAINT OF TOXIC LOYALTY

Now let's switch it up.

Jezebel was married to Ahab, the King of Israel. He was powerful—but pitiful. Emotionally fragile, spiritually bankrupt, and petty on his best day.

Case in point: Ahab wanted a man's vineyard. The man said no—because it was his inheritance, a sacred legacy. Ahab went home, sulked like a toddler denied a Happy Meal, and refused to eat.

So Jezebel did what she always did: weaponized her position.

She forged letters in Ahab's name, falsely accused the vineyard owner, and had him killed. She cleaned her hands and handed the vineyard to her sulking husband like it was a Valentine's Day gift.

All for a man too weak to hear "no."

Jezebel's loyalty was lethal. She empowered Ahab's worst instincts. She didn't challenge his foolishness—she enabled it, expanded it, and eventually died because of it.

She was thrown out a window and eaten by dogs. Let that visual stay with you.

Abigail vs. Jezebel: The Comparison Table

Feature	Abigail	Jezebel
Husband	Foolish and rude	Foolish and passive
Approach	Intervenes with wisdom	Interferes with wickedness
Motivation	Protect her household and honor	Preserve power and control
Outcome	Marries a future king	Dies violently, name becomes an insult
Legacy	Woman of discernment	Symbol of corruption

MODERN PARALLELS: ARE YOU COVERING OR CODDLING?

Let's bring this home. Every woman in a relationship with a foolish man makes a choice:

1. **Cover wisely** like Abigail—without enabling.

2. **Coddle dangerously** like Jezebel—and become complicit in his collapse.

Modern-day Abigails are the wives who step in, not to clean up the mess, but to stop the explosion. They set boundaries. They speak truth —even when it's risky. They protect the future, not just the feelings.

Modern-day Jezebels? They spin the narrative, do damage control, silence truth-tellers, and gaslight anybody who threatens their illusion of control.

And the men? Oh, they're everywhere. From the Nabal in your group chat who thinks a meme is a love language... to the Ahab at your family barbecue, still mad someone told him he couldn't be the DJ.

A.R.K. APPLICATION:

- **Acknowledgment**: Are you pretending everything is fine because you're scared of the fallout?

- **Respect**: Are you demanding respect for your role while excusing disrespect from your partner?

- **Known**: Do you feel like your wisdom is invisible while his stupidity is on display?

REFLECTION QUESTIONS

- Which wife do you identify with more right now—Abigail or Jezebel?

- Have you ever tried to "save" someone by compromising your integrity?

- What's one area where you need to stop coddling foolishness?

FINAL WORD

Stupidity isn't just in what they do—it's in what we allow.

You don't have to go down with a fool just because you married one, dated one, or voted for one.

You have choices. You have power. You have wisdom.

Be the Abigail.

Not the accessory to a disaster.

2

THE TALE OF TWO HUSBANDS

ADAM VS. JOB

"The wrong silence can be louder than any lie."

— ANONYMOUS, BUT IT SOUNDS LIKE SOMETHING
EVE WHISPERED UNDER HER BREATH

TWO HUSBANDS. TWO WIVES. TWO VERY DIFFERENT OUTCOMES.

We've all seen it: the man who won't speak up, and the man who refuses to shut up. But in this chapter, we're not dealing with loudness—we're dealing with **responses**. How do men respond when their partner makes a questionable choice? Or when the pressure is on? That's what separates **Adam** from **Job**.

Let's start in Eden... and end at the ash heap.

ADAM: THE FIRST HUSBAND, THE FIRST ENABLER

Ah, Adam. The original "go-along-to-get-along" guy. The man who had one command and still fumbled the assignment.

God gave Adam instructions **directly**—don't eat from that one tree. That's it. No fine print. No loopholes. Just "don't touch the fruit."

But when Eve—his wife, his rib, his ride-or-die—ate the fruit and handed it to him, Adam didn't say a word. No questions. No pause. No spiritual pushback.

He bit into that forbidden fruit like it was the Sunday brunch special.

And when God came calling? Oh, now Adam finds his voice:

"The woman you gave me..."

The audacity.

Instead of taking accountability, he played the blame game with both God and Eve. Classic deflection. And it didn't just cost him his garden—it cost humanity paradise.

Adam's silence in the moment and blame afterward tell us something deep: *passivity in the face of foolishness is still participation.*

Modern Adams are everywhere. Quiet while you destroy your peace. Silent while you unravel. Watching you spiral and calling it "support." They don't challenge you because they fear your reaction—or worse, they don't care enough to confront.

JOB: THE SUFFERING SAINT WHO STILL HAD SENSE

Now Job? Job was built differently.

This man lost everything: children, wealth, health, and respect. He was covered in sores, scraping his skin with broken pottery, surrounded by friends who sounded more like frenemies.

And then came his wife.

She saw his suffering and famously told him:

"Curse God and die."

Yikes.

Now here's where Job shows us something powerful. He doesn't curse her. He doesn't obey her. He doesn't call the divorce lawyer or throw a sandal.

He simply says:

"You speak as one of the foolish women speaks."

Pause and admire that response. He didn't call her foolish—he called out the *behavior*. He held the line without losing compassion. He spoke truth **with restraint**.

Modern-day Jobs are rare—but they exist. Men who can hear foolishness without amplifying it. Men who can correct with love. Men who suffer but don't let their pain justify foolish decisions.

Adam vs. Job: A Breakdown

Feature	Adam	Job
Situation	Wife makes poor choice	Wife gives reckless advice
Response	Silent, then blame	Calm correction with boundaries
Accountability	Deflected	Maintained personal integrity
Outcome	Expelled from Eden	Restored double by God
Legacy	Passive partner	Faithful under pressure

MODERN-DAY HUSBANDS: PASSIVE VS. PURPOSEFUL

In relationships today, we still see this tension. The man who won't speak up when his wife is sliding into foolishness... and the man who can lovingly check her without condemnation.

A modern Adam says:

- "Whatever makes you happy."

- "I didn't want to argue."

- "You do you, babe."

A modern Job says:

- "I love you, but that's not wise."

- "I'm not going to co-sign that."

- "We're better than this."

And ladies, before you get too comfortable: ask yourself—do you want a man who'll cosign your chaos? Or one who'll lovingly stop you from self-sabotage?

A.R.K. APPLICATION:

- **Acknowledgment**: Are you recognizing when silence is damaging?

- **Respect**: Are you holding space for correction—or demanding blind loyalty?

- **Known**: Do you feel truly seen by your partner, or just pacified?

REFLECTION QUESTIONS

- Have you ever been more like Adam—silent and complicit?

- Do you know someone who "Job'd" you—called out your foolishness with love?

- How do you respond when someone challenges you with truth?

FINAL WORD

Not every man who loves you will *lead* you.

Not every man who stays silent is *safe*.

Sometimes the real danger isn't what he says... it's what he refuses to say.

In a world full of Adams, find yourself a Job.

And if you've been an Adam? Don't panic. Just start speaking truth— even when it's hard.

Because love without accountability is just enabling in a tuxedo.

3

DELILAH & SAMSON

BEAUTY, BICEPS, AND BAD DECISIONS

"When you confuse intensity with intimacy, you'll always end up in bondage."

— *THE FRIEND WHO BEGGED YOU NOT TO TEXT HIM BACK*

WHEN LOOKS KILL (COMMON SENSE)

Let's talk about the ultimate "he was fine, but..." story. Samson —the original gym bro of the Bible. Muscles on muscles. Called and chosen by God. A literal Nazarite with supernatural strength, destined to deliver Israel from the Philistines.

But despite the divine calling and power, Samson had a fatal weakness: **women who didn't want him to win.**

And at the top of that list? **Delilah.**

Delilah was beautiful, persuasive, and calculating. She wasn't here for love—she was here for leverage. She was the kind of woman who'll stroke your ego while secretly selling your secrets.

Let's break this down.

SAMSON: STRONG IN BODY, WEAK IN BOUNDARIES

Samson was called to be set apart. But his desire for what looked good to him consistently overrode what was *good for him*. Over and over, he chose women from enemy nations—women who didn't respect his purpose or honor his identity.

Delilah was the final straw.

She was approached by the Philistine rulers and offered a fat bag to discover the secret of Samson's strength. And like a toxic partner playing the long game, she wore him down with questions, guilt trips, and manipulation.

"If you loved me, you'd tell me."

"Why don't you trust me?"

"You're making me look stupid in front of my friends!"

Sound familiar?

Samson resisted—at first. He gave false answers. He dodged the question. But Delilah was persistent. She didn't want the man—she wanted what the man *carried*.

And eventually... he folded.

He told her everything. The vow. The hair. The strength. And what did Delilah do?

She **put him to sleep on her lap,** called the Philistines, and had his head shaved clean like a baby's bottom.

When Samson woke up, the Bible says:

"He did not know that the Lord had left him."

Whew. That'll preach.

DELILAH: THE BLUEPRINT FOR BETRAYAL

Delilah never lied about who she was. She was transactional from the start. But Samson? He was the fool who thought lust could be loyalty.

She was offered silver, and she took it. She was given a mission, and she executed it. No love. No loyalty. Just ambition in a satin robe.

Modern-day Delilahs aren't always obvious. They flirt with your potential while planning your fall. They post your best moments but secretly hope you fail. They don't want *you*—they want the clout, the control, the story.

Delilah didn't just cut hair—she cut purpose.

Samson & Delilah: The Breakdown

Feature	Samson	Delilah
Strength	Physical, divine	Emotional manipulation
Motivation	Connection, desire	Control, compensation
Weakness	Lack of discernment	Lack of integrity
Outcome	Lost strength, captured	Gained money, lost soul
Legacy	Tragic potential	Symbol of betrayal

MODERN PARALLELS: WHO'S IN YOUR LAP?

Let's not act like this was a one-time biblical event. This is still happening every day:

- Falling for fine over faithful.

- Sharing secrets with people who screenshot and snitch.

- Ignoring red flags because the sex is fire and they "get you."

Modern-day Samson isn't just in the gym—he's in the DMs, thinking with biceps instead of wisdom.

Modern-day Delilahs come in all genders. They know your weakness. They see your gift. And instead of protecting it, they exploit it.

And sometimes? *You* are the Delilah... using affection as a weapon because you're mad at the world.

A.R.K. APPLICATION:

- **Acknowledgment**: Are you pretending your situationship is real love?

- **Respect**: Are you allowing someone to violate your boundaries because you're afraid to be alone?

- **Known**: Does your partner *really* know your value—or just how to drain it?

REFLECTION QUESTIONS

- Have you ever shared too much with someone who didn't deserve your trust?

- Are you sleeping in the lap of someone who doesn't pray for your strength?

- Are you ignoring God's purpose for you because you're addicted to being wanted?

FINAL WORD

Love shouldn't leave you bald, blind, and bound.

Discernment is sexy. Wisdom is power. And boundaries? They're holy.

Don't let your anointing be auctioned off for attention.

Don't let Delilah put you to sleep while your destiny is on the line.

Your purpose is too valuable to be pillow talk.

4

DAVID & BATHSHEBA

WHEN POWER BLINDS MORALITY

"Just because they have a title doesn't mean they have character."

*— SAID EVERY PERSON WHO EVER TRUSTED A
LEADER TOO MUCH*

POWERFUL MEN. PASSIVE WOMEN. PERMANENT
CONSEQUENCES.

David is known as "a man after God's own heart," but Chapter 4 reminds us he was also a man after another man's wife. The story of David and Bathsheba isn't a love story—it's a cautionary tale. One about power, privilege, and how sin multiplies when it's left unchecked.

David wasn't just some guy. He was the **king**. The same David who took down Goliath, wrote Psalms, and danced before the Lord with all his might... also manipulated his power to steal, deceive, and kill.

And Bathsheba? She was caught in the middle. Her voice is barely heard in scripture, but her body became the battlefield of a moral collapse.

DAVID: THE KING WHO TOOK WHAT HE WANTED

It was spring—when kings go to war—but David stayed home. That detail is important. Because when leaders get idle, their eyes start wandering.

From his rooftop, David spotted Bathsheba bathing. He didn't *accidentally* see her. He looked, lingered, and lusted. Then he asked about her—found out she was married—and sent for her anyway.

Bathsheba came. Did she have a choice? Debate continues. But when the king calls you in a patriarchal society, saying no isn't exactly an option.

She got pregnant. David panicked.

Instead of owning his mistake, he tried to cover it. He brought her husband, Uriah, home from war and encouraged him to "spend time with his wife." Uriah refused—he had too much integrity to relax while his men were fighting.

So David sent Uriah back to battle with a sealed letter containing his own death sentence. Uriah died. David married Bathsheba. Problem solved... right?

Wrong.

God saw it all.

And when the prophet Nathan came with a parable and a mirror, David finally broke.

BATHSHEBA: THE SILENCED AND THE SEEN

Bathsheba doesn't get much dialogue in scripture. She is acted upon, but rarely heard from.

But her story is not insignificant. She represents the many women who are:

- Used but not loved.

- Named but not known.

- Blamed for the sins of men with power.

She lost a child. Lived with shame. But later, through divine grace and restoration, became the mother of **Solomon**, one of the wisest men to ever live.

From pain came purpose—but it never justified the path.

David & Bathsheba: The Breakdown

Feature	David	Bathsheba
Role	King, chosen by God	Wife, powerless in system
Action	Lusts, takes, covers up	Responds to command
Accountability	Initially hides, then repents	Suffers quietly
Outcome	Child dies, legacy preserved	Becomes mother to Solomon
Legacy	Flawed leader, deeply loved	Silenced woman, spiritually significant

MODERN PARALLELS: WHEN LEADERSHIP GOES LEFT

We've all seen it:

- The boss who abuses authority.

- The pastor who preaches purity but texts inappropriately.

- The partner who says, "God told me you're my wife," after 3 DMs and zero boundaries.

David's story reminds us that **calling doesn't cancel accountability**.

And Bathsheba? She's the woman in the boardroom, the choir stand, or the office kitchen—navigating systems that weren't built to protect her.

A.R.K. APPLICATION:

- **Acknowledgment**: Are you excusing power plays because they come with praise?

- **Respect**: Are you respecting others' boundaries—or manipulating them?

- **Known**: Are you in a relationship where your voice disappears the moment their title shows up?

REFLECTION QUESTIONS

- Have you ever used your position or influence to get your way?

- Have you ever felt like Bathsheba—pulled into something without being heard?

- Are you confusing repentance with damage control?

FINAL WORD

God can restore what sin tries to ruin—but He doesn't skip the consequences.

Being powerful doesn't make you wise.

Being desired doesn't mean you're valued.

Being chosen doesn't mean you're exempt from correction.

Let David remind you:

Just because it's possible doesn't mean it's permissible.

And just because you got away with it... doesn't mean God didn't see it.

PART II
MODERN STUPIDITY

SAME SCRIPTS, NEW ACTORS

5

THE TALE OF TANISHA AND TYRONE

"HE GOT POTENTIAL THOUGH"

"Don't fall in love with potential. Potential never paid a bill, healed a wound, or showed up on time."

— *SOMEBODY'S GRANDMA, TIRED OF WATCHING YOU CRY*

THE MODERN-DAY RELATIONSHIP BLUEPRINT FOR BURNOUT

Tanisha had a plan: build a life, grow a business, maybe get married by 35. She was smart, ambitious, the kind of woman who kept a vision board, a prayer journal, and a backup charger in her purse. She was ready for partnership.

Then she met **Tyrone.**

He had charm, good teeth, a smooth playlist, and just enough trauma to make her feel like she was on a healing mission. He wasn't consistent—but he had *potential*. And to Tanisha, that was enough.

For a while.

TYRONE: MR. ALMOST

Tyrone wasn't abusive. He wasn't evil. But he was *exhausting*.

He'd talk about starting a business—but never register the LLC.

He'd post motivational quotes—but couldn't hold a job.

He knew all the love languages—but weaponized them when things didn't go his way.

He didn't lie—he just didn't follow through.

He had big plans. Big dreams. Big declarations. And Tanisha believed him—because he believed himself. But belief doesn't pay rent. And dreams don't fix disrespect.

TANISHA: THE LOYAL VISIONARY

Tanisha saw what Tyrone could be. She stuck around through inconsistency, ghosting, and the occasional "I'm going through something" text.

She prayed for him. Waited on him. Covered for him with friends.

She defended his absences, his delays, and his hot-and-cold energy.

Every time he failed to show up, she wrote it off as:

- "He's just overwhelmed."

- "He's never had someone love him like this."

- "He just needs time."

And let's be clear: *she wasn't stupid*. She was **hopeful**. And hope is a hell of a drug.

THE TURNING POINT

It wasn't one big moment that broke her. It was the slow erosion:

- The canceled plans.

- The borrowed money.

- The excuses.

- The birthdays missed and the gaslighting that followed.

She looked in the mirror one day and didn't recognize herself. Her sparkle was dimmed. Her joy was muted. Her life was on *pause*— waiting on someone who never pressed "play."

And that's when she realized: **potential is only attractive when it's paired with progress**.

Tanisha & Tyrone: The Breakdown

Feature	Tanisha	Tyrone
Motivation	Build together	Be supported without building
Conflict Style	Defend and delay	Withdraw and deflect
Love Language	Acts of service and patience	Words of affirmation (and none of the work)
Outcome	Emotional burnout	Delayed accountability
Legacy	Grew through grief	Floated on charm

MODERN PARALLEL: THE RELATIONSHIP RESUME

Tyrone had the résumé of a dream partner... if only interviews were based on vibes. He talked about healing but avoided therapy. He talked about loyalty but flirted with his ex. He gave just enough to keep her hoping, not enough to keep her whole.

And Tanisha? She fell into the most common trap of all: **dating potential and ignoring patterns**.

A.R.K. APPLICATION:

- **Acknowledgment:** Are you calling it "potential" because you don't want to admit you're scared to start over?

- **Respect:** Are you getting crumbs and calling it a feast?

- **Known:** Does this person really see you—or just see how much you can carry for them?

REFLECTION QUESTIONS

- Have you ever confused "growth" with "waiting around"?

- What have you sacrificed while holding out hope?

- If your best friend were dating your partner—would you be worried?

FINAL WORD

Staying with someone because of their *potential* is like investing in a house you're not allowed to renovate.

Love requires movement. Growth. Effort.

You can't date "future him" and live with "present mess."

You deserve a partner, not a project.

Let go of the fantasy long enough to see the facts.

And remember: **God didn't call you to be a life coach with benefits.**

6

KEISHA AND THE CHURCH OF WHAT'S CONVENIENT

"Some people don't want a relationship with God. They want a religion that cosigns their dysfunction."

— *THE FRIEND WHO LEFT THE GROUP CHAT AFTER*
THAT ONE BIBLE STUDY

WHEN FAITH IS A COVER FOR FOOLISHNESS

Keisha loved God. She grew up in the front pew, baptized at 12, junior usher board, Sabbath (Sunday)school scholar, and a praise dance ministry regular. She knew scripture, quoted Psalms like song lyrics, and never missed communion—even when she missed sleep.

But somewhere along the way, Keisha confused **performance** with **presence**. And in her search for healing, community, and love, she ran smack into the arms of the *Church of What's Convenient*—a ministry where appearances mattered more than accountability, and silence was called "submission."

THE CHURCH THAT LOVED THE IMAGE... AND IGNORED THE ISSUE

The pastor said "marriage is ministry," but never mentioned that ministry shouldn't feel like martyrdom. Keisha was in a relationship that drained her. Her man was in the church—but not in Christ. He had the language, the lingo, the limp from "wrestling with God"... but no fruit.

He served on five ministries, but couldn't manage his temper.

He quoted Proverbs but couldn't communicate.

He prayed in public, but stonewalled in private.

And when Keisha finally went to the church mothers for advice, they told her:

- "Girl, just keep praying."

- "The devil is busy."

- "Don't let the enemy steal your blessing."

They made her feel like her pain was a test... instead of a signal.

KEISHA: FAITHFUL BUT FRUSTRATED

Keisha started questioning herself:

Was she not spiritual enough? Did she dishonor him by asking for emotional safety? Was her frustration a lack of faith?

No. Her frustration was **wisdom trying to wake her up**.

She wasn't "lacking submission." She was suffocating under spiritual gaslighting.

What she needed was **permission to leave a situation that wasn't God's best**, not pressure to stay and perform faith like it was a Broadway show.

THE CONVENIENT GOSPEL

Let's talk real: the **Convenient Gospel** is the version of church culture that:

- Excuses bad behavior because "he's a man of God."

- Tells women to be quiet, be sweet, and be strong —simultaneously.

- Rewards survival, not healing.

It's a gospel that quotes Ephesians 5:22 about wives submitting... but forgets verse 25 about husbands loving like Christ, who *died* for the church, not manipulated it.

Keisha & The Church: The Breakdown

Feature	Keisha	The Church (in this story)
Desire	Spiritual partnership	Image maintenance
Challenge	Being emotionally neglected	Being held accountable
Support Given	Pray harder, submit more	Minimal, moralistic advice
Outcome	Religious exhaustion	Maintained dysfunction

MODERN PARALLEL: SANCTIFIED BUT STILL SUFFERING

So many Keishas are in pews today:

- Leading small groups while bleeding internally.

- Raising families while shrinking themselves.

- Smiling in selfies with a spouse they're scared of spiritually or emotionally.

And too often, churches respond to their pain with **theological gaslighting**, dressed up in pretty words like "season," "assignment," or "breakthrough."

Sometimes your breakthrough is in **walking away**, not in *waiting it out*.

A.R.K. APPLICATION:

- **Acknowledgment**: Are you pretending your relationship is a testimony when it's really a trauma bond?

- **Respect**: Do your spiritual leaders respect your need for emotional health—or just your willingness to serve?

- **Known**: Are you known for your gifting or your growth? Your platform or your pain?

REFLECTION QUESTIONS

- Have you ever stayed in a relationship because "the church said so"?

- Are you confusing loyalty to a person or system with loyalty to God?

- What does freedom in Christ actually *look* like in your relationships?

FINAL WORD

Faith should not be a prison.

Submission should not feel like suffocation.

And staying with someone who's spiritually lazy isn't *godly*—it's codependency wrapped in a Bible verse.

Keisha's faith was never the problem.

The *interpretation* of it was.

So if you need permission to stop performing for people and start living in truth?

Here it is.

7

POLITICAL STUPID

WHEN VOTING AGAINST YOUR OWN INTEREST BECOMES A LIFESTYLE

"Every time you vote against your own best interest, a billionaire gets his wings."

— THE GHOST OF COMMON SENSE, WEEPING SOFTLY INTO A BALLOT BOX

THE POLITICS OF DELUSION

There's a special kind of foolishness that happens every election cycle.

People step into the voting booth with a Bible in one hand, a Facebook meme in the other, and absolutely no awareness that the policy they're voting for will make their rent higher, their rights fewer, and their healthcare more expensive.

And then they get shocked.

Shocked when gas prices rise.

Shocked when their reproductive rights vanish.

Shocked when the same people they elected gut their pensions, ban their books, and cut their benefits.

But don't worry—they've still got "family values" and prayer in school, right?

THE TRAP OF IMAGE OVER IMPACT

The problem isn't that people don't care.

It's that they care about **how things look** more than how they actually *are*.

So they vote for the "Christian candidate" who hasn't opened a Bible since 1987.

They support the "pro-family" bill that cuts funding for actual families.

They choose the tax plan that benefits billionaires because *one day* they might be rich too.

It's aspirational stupidity.

It's voting like you're the CEO—when you can't even get PTO.

THE CULT OF PERSONALITY

Let's talk about it.

Some folks don't vote based on policy.

They vote based on *personality*—and not even the real one. Just the TV edit. The charisma. The soundbites. The "he tells it like it is" vibe, even if "it" is dangerous, ignorant, or outright hateful.

They confuse arrogance for strength.

They confuse volume for leadership.

They confuse tweets for truth.

And when it all falls apart? They double down. Because **admitting you got played feels worse than staying wrong.**

WHY WE STAY STUPID (EVEN WHEN WE KNOW BETTER)

Sometimes it's pride.

Sometimes it's tradition.

Sometimes it's because "my daddy voted this way, and his daddy before him..."

But other times? It's because we're so conditioned to survive dysfunction that we can't imagine what thriving would even look like.

We settle for scraps and call it stability.

YOU CAN'T PRAY YOUR WAY OUT OF A POLICY YOU VOTED IN

This is where it gets real.

You can't vote for leaders who gut your community and then cry for revival.

You can't support laws that hurt your neighbors and then claim to love Jesus.

You can't ask for miracles when you *keep electing Pharaoh*.

Sometimes your suffering isn't a test—**it's a result.**

Political Stupid: The Breakdown

Symptom	Belief	Reality
Values Over Vitality	"They're pro-life!"	Until the baby's born and needs healthcare
Identity Voting	"He's one of us!"	He's one of them. You just own the merch.
Economic Gaslighting	"Trickle-down works!"	It trickles nowhere but up.
Misplaced Loyalty	"My party right or wrong."	Wrong is still wrong.
Evangelical Exceptionalism	"This is a Christian nation."	Then why does it look nothing like Christ?

A.R.K. APPLICATION:

- **Acknowledgment**: Are you ignoring how your vote impacts people who don't look like you?

- **Respect**: Do you respect your neighbor's dignity—or just your party's talking points?

- **Known**: Are you known for compassion... or compliance?

REFLECTION QUESTIONS

- Have you ever voted for someone out of fear instead of hope?

- Do you know the actual policies of the people you support—or just the vibes?

- Are you willing to admit when you got it wrong?

Final Word

Voting is sacred.

But it's not magic.

It's not holy just because someone quoted a Bible verse at a rally.

It's not right just because it's legal.

You are not obligated to stay loyal to ignorance.

You are allowed to outgrow your party, your family's habits, and your own past votes.

Because stupidity doesn't care who you voted for.

It just loves when you stay comfortable... and quiet.

This isn't about Republican or Democrat.

This is about waking up before your rights are all gone and your regrets are all that's left.

So next time you vote—vote like your freedom depends on it.

Because it does.

8

LOVE IS NOT SUPPOSED TO HURT...REPEATEDLY

"If love keeps making you cry, it's not love—it's a warning."

— *THE THERAPIST YOU SHOULD'VE LISTENED TO*
TWO HEARTBREAKS AGO

THE ROMANCE OF SUFFERING

Somewhere along the line, many of us were taught that love = sacrifice. And sacrifice = pain. And pain = proof that it's real.

We were told to "ride or die."

To "stick it out."

To "hold him down."

To "be his peace."

Even if he was our storm.

We saw our mothers tolerate cheating, our aunties forgive disrespect, our friends romanticize being emotionally unavailable—and we thought, *this must be what love looks like.*

Spoiler alert: It's not.

THE MYTH OF STRUGGLE LOVE

Struggle love is the kind of relationship that runs on fumes, forgiveness, and fantasy. It thrives on one good week after three bad ones. It feeds on your hope and starves your joy.

It's when you stay because:

- "We've been through so much."

- "I know he loves me deep down."

- "It's just a phase."

- "Nobody's perfect."

But what you don't realize is—you're bleeding, and calling it bonding.

You're anchoring yourself to a ship that's been sinking for years, and mistaking your endurance for divine purpose.

THE EMOTIONAL GYMNASTICS OF STAYING

When you're in struggle love, you start adjusting everything:

- Your boundaries shrink.

- Your expectations lower.

- Your standards bend until they break.

You do mental gymnastics to justify the behavior:

- "He didn't mean it like that."

- "She's just going through something."

- "Maybe I'm too sensitive."

No, you're not. You're just waking up.

BUT WHAT ABOUT LOYALTY?

Loyalty isn't about how long you suffer.

It's about how aligned your values stay.

And sometimes, staying loyal to them means being disloyal to yourself.

If you have to betray your peace to prove your commitment—it's not love. It's *emotional manipulation*.

THE PRICE OF STAYING TOO LONG

Staying in a relationship that hurts you isn't noble. It's costly:

- You lose time.

- You lose self-worth.

- You lose clarity.

And by the time you leave (if you leave), you're not just walking away from the person—you're recovering from the *version of yourself* you became to survive them.

Struggle Love: The Breakdown

Feature	What It Looks Like	What It Costs You
Drama Cycles	Breakup, makeup, rinse, repeat	Emotional fatigue
Inconsistent Effort	Grand gestures after neglect	Confused expectations
Guilt as Glue	Staying because "they need me"	Loss of self and joy
Spiritual Baggage	"God wants me to stay and pray"	Confusing faith with enabling
Social Pressure	"We look good together"	Embarrassment when truth unravels

A.R.K. APPLICATION:

- **Acknowledgment**: Are you honest about how much this relationship is hurting you?

- **Respect**: Do you feel respected in both your silence and your voice?

- **Known**: Are you known as you *are*, or only tolerated when you shrink?

REFLECTION QUESTIONS

- Do you mistake intensity for intimacy?

- Have you been taught that love is proven by how much pain you can endure?

- What would love look like if it didn't hurt?

FINAL WORD

Love isn't supposed to hurt over and over again.

It's not supposed to leave you anxious, afraid, or empty.

It's not a test of your threshold for abuse. It's a reflection of your understanding of *worth*.

You don't have to prove you're worthy of love by surviving dysfunction.

You don't need to bleed to be chosen.

And you sure don't have to suffer to be seen.

Love doesn't hurt. Trauma does.

Gaslighting does. Immaturity does. Narcissism does.

You deserve soft.

You deserve steady.

You deserve love that feels like healing—not harm.

PART III
THE STUPIDITY SPECTRUM

SIGNS, STAGES, AND SOLUTIONS

9

THE SIGNS YOU'RE DATING STUPID (OR BEING STUPID)

"If you're asking everyone but God whether you should stay, you already have your answer."

— *THE COUSIN WHO GHOSTED HER TOXIC EX AND NEVER LOOKED BACK*

LET'S BE HONEST

Y ou know when something's off. You know when it doesn't feel right. But you ignore it. You pray about it. You journal around it. You ask your group chat hoping *someone* will say, "Girl, it's probably nothing."

And sometimes they do.

Because they're being polite.

Because they're tired of hearing about him.

Or because they're in stupid situationships of their own.

But not today. Today we're naming the signs.

And if it stings? That's just truth doing what truth does.

RED FLAG RUNDOWN: A LIST YOU CAN'T UNSEE

► They're Consistent at Being Inconsistent

If their energy, effort, and emotional availability come in cycles, but they're always consistent when it comes to *excuses*—you're dating stupid.

► You're Always Explaining Your Worth

If you have to *convince* someone to treat you like you matter, you're not in a relationship—you're in an audition.

► Their Apologies Come With Amnesia

They say "I'm sorry" but act brand new every time they do the same thing again. That's not repentance. That's rehearsal.

► You Make Excuses for Them to Other People

If every sentence starts with "Well, what had happened was..."—you're not protecting them, you're prolonging your pain.

► Your Gut Is Screaming, But Your Hope Is Louder

If your body is tense, your spirit is tired, and your heart feels like it's on probation—*that ain't peace, sis.*

AND THEN THERE'S YOU...

Let's not just talk about *them*. Let's talk about **you.**

You might be acting a little stupid too if:

- You stay because *"they have potential."*

- You've googled "How to make them commit" more than once.

- You're in a full relationship... in your mind.

- You've broken up with them in your head—but not in real life.

Let's call it what it is: **You're avoiding clarity because clarity requires change.**

The Relationship Stupidity Spectrum

Let's chart it out, shall we?

Level	Description	Example
Mild	"They just need time."	Waiting for someone who's not waiting for you
Moderate	"They didn't mean it like that."	Justifying red flags with childhood trauma
Severe	"But when it's good, it's SO good."	Excusing abuse because of make-up moments
Terminal	"God told me to stay and suffer."	Confusing toxic patterns with spiritual tests

A.R.K. APPLICATION:

- **Acknowledgment**: Are you ignoring reality because fantasy feels better?

- **Respect**: Are you respecting yourself, or just hoping they'll start?

- **Known**: Do they actually know the real you—or just the version you perform to keep them around?

REFLECTION QUESTIONS

- What red flag have you explained away more than three times?

- Who are you trying to prove your worth to—and why?

- If you left this relationship today, what would you gain?

FINAL WORD

Stupid doesn't always show up wearing a sign.

Sometimes it shows up with flowers, good sex, spiritual language, and "Let's just see where this goes."

But make no mistake—stupid is still stupid.

And love will never require you to lose your mind to keep someone's attention.

If you're dating stupid... step away.

And if you're being stupid? Grace is available.

You can always choose differently.

Don't be loyal to your own confusion.

10

THE JUSTIFICATION OLYMPICS
GOLD MEDALS IN GASLIGHTING

"If you have to explain it more than twice, it's not a relationship—it's a debate club."

— *THE THERAPIST WHO NOW ONLY TAKES CASH BECAUSE Y'ALL WORE HER OUT WITH EXCUSES*

WELCOME TO THE GAMES

There should be a whole section in the Olympics for emotional gymnastics.

Events include:

- **The Vault of Denial**

- **The Floor Routine of Excuses**

- **The Synchronized "But He Had a Rough Childhood" Routine**

- **The Triple Twist of "It's Not That Serious"**

And if you stick the landing with a tearful "I just love them so much," you might even qualify for **nationals**.

LET'S BE REAL

We've all done it.

Made excuses for people who don't deserve the stage time.

Rationalized red flags like we're their defense attorney.

Wrote entire essays in our heads about why the thing they did wasn't *that bad.*

Because if we don't justify it... we'd have to leave.

We'd have to change.

We'd have to admit we stayed too long, gave too much, or believed too hard.

And sometimes that truth feels harder than the lie.

POPULAR JUSTIFICATIONS (THAT AIN'T JUSTIFYING A THING)

🏅 "They Had a Tough Childhood"

Yes. And that's valid. But **so did you**—and you're not out here manipulating people or ghosting them after they open their heart.

🥈 "They're Not Like This All the Time"

Right. Because abusers and manipulators know how to behave just long enough to reset your hope.

🥉 "We've Been Through So Much Together"

A shared trauma does not equal shared purpose. You didn't bond—you trauma-bonded.

Honorable Mention: "God Told Me to Stay"

Sis. God also gave you **wisdom, boundaries, and peace** as a fruit of the Spirit—not *high blood pressure and voice notes that sound like hostage videos.*

HOW GASLIGHTING HOOKS YOU

Gaslighting doesn't just come from the other person.

It's the internal voice that rewrites history so you can stay comfortable.

Examples:

- *"Maybe I overreacted..."*

- *"Maybe I'm too sensitive..."*

- *"Maybe they're right—I'm the problem."*

When you're constantly doubting your reality, you become easy to control—not just by them, but by your own fear of being alone.

SELF-GASLIGHTING IS A THING, TOO

You know how it goes:

- You feel something's off.

- You confront it.

- They deny it.

- You backpedal.

- And now *you're* apologizing for bringing it up.

Congratulations—you just self-gaslit. You turned your own intuition into an inconvenience.

Justification Olympics: The Breakdown

Excuse	Root Fear	Reality Check
"It's not that bad."	Fear of being alone	If you have to say this often—it is.
"They'll change."	Fear of wasted time	Hope without action is a delay tactic.
"I'm not perfect."	Fear of confrontation	You don't have to be perfect to be respected.
"We have history."	Fear of starting over	History can be sacred—and still be over.

A.R.K. APPLICATION:

- **Acknowledgment**: What lie are you telling yourself to make this situation feel survivable?

- **Respect**: Are you justifying behavior you'd never accept from a stranger?

- **Known**: Are you staying because they know you—or because they've studied how to manipulate you?

REFLECTION QUESTIONS

- What's the biggest excuse you've made in this relationship?

- What would it look like to believe your own feelings the *first* time?

- Who benefits from you shrinking your standards?

FINAL WORD

Gaslighting isn't just someone else's tactic—it can become *your* survival strategy.

Justifying someone else's dysfunction doesn't make you loyal.

It makes you tired.

Stop defending behavior that's draining you.

Stop explaining the same disappointment with new vocabulary.

Stop calling it love when it's really **emotional taxation**.

And if you're going to compete in anything?

Compete in healing. Win gold in boundaries. And break records in self-respect.

WHEN YOUR INNER CHILD
LOVES A CLOWN

"If your wound is choosing your partner, don't be surprised when the relationship becomes a bandage that won't stick."

— *THE HEALED VERSION OF YOU, BEGGING YOU TO*
PICK PEACE

LET'S TALK ABOUT HER—THE INNER CHILD

The version of you who:

- Didn't get enough affection.

- Was told to be strong before you were fully seen.

- Thought attention—even toxic attention—was proof of love.

She's still in there.

And sometimes, *she's the one swiping right.*

Not grown you. Not healed you.

But wounded you.

Abandoned you.

"Please pick me" you.

And baby, she loves a clown. Because clowns are entertaining. They show up big. They fill the silence. They promise laughter. And most of all... they remind her of **home**, even if home was chaotic.

THE PSYCHOLOGY OF CHOOSING A CIRCUS

When your nervous system is wired for survival—not stability—you start confusing:

- **Adrenaline** with affection.

- **Drama** with depth.

- **Unpredictability** with passion.

If your childhood love was conditional, erratic, or performative, you may chase those same dynamics now—not because they feel good, but because they feel *familiar.*

And what feels familiar feels safe... even when it's harmful.

SPOTTING THE CLOWN YOU CHOSE

Let's break it down. The clown:

- **Love bombs** you with over-the-top affection... then disappears.

- **Jokes** when it's time to have hard conversations.

- **Performs** vulnerability but never follows through with growth.

- **Turns every confrontation into a comedy special**—so you stop trying to be serious.

And your inner child laughs. Because she thinks if she's fun enough, forgiving enough, flexible enough... she'll finally be loved back.

But what she really needs is **to be reparented by you**—the grown version who knows love should feel like peace, not a punchline.

HEALING IS LEARNING TO SAY: "I DON'T DATE CLOWNS NO MORE"

You don't need another man who can juggle your emotions.

You don't need another woman who pulls rabbits out of hats but disappears when it's time to be accountable.

You don't need someone who makes you laugh until you cry—because you're the only one doing the crying.

You need safety. Stillness. **Sanity.**

Inner Child Love vs. Adult Love: The Breakdown

Inner Child Says...	Healed Adult Knows...
"I just want them to choose me."	"I choose myself—even when they won't."
"I can fix them."	"I can support you, but I won't save you."
"If I love them enough, they'll stay."	"Healthy love doesn't need convincing."
"They didn't mean it."	"Intent doesn't erase impact."
"It's my fault."	"It's not my job to carry their chaos."

A.R.K. APPLICATION:

- **Acknowledgment**: What part of you is still trying to earn love through pain?

- **Respect**: Do you respect yourself enough to disappoint your trauma?

- **Known**: Are you choosing partners who see the real you—or just the wounded version trying to prove your worth?

REFLECTION QUESTIONS

- What's the earliest memory you have of confusing love with approval?

- What kind of "clown" are you still attracted to?

- What would your healed self say to your younger self about love?

FINAL WORD

There's a little girl inside of you who got stuck chasing people who made her feel small just to feel seen.

She thought chaos meant she was chosen.

She thought neglect meant she needed to try harder.

But now?

You're grown.

You're healing.

You're whole—or on your way.

And it's time to show your inner child that she doesn't have to fall in love with the circus anymore.

Because real love doesn't require a red nose, a tightrope, or an audience.

Real love is soft, steady, and doesn't disappear when the laughter stops.

12

CO-STARRING IN THEIR CIRCUS

THE ART OF NOT BEING THE FOOL

"Not my monkey, not my circus."

— ANCIENT WISDOM PASSED DOWN BY
EXHAUSTED EMPATHS EVERYWHERE

SO HERE'S THE SCENE...

They have the main character energy.

The drama.

The chaos.

The sob story.

The trauma plotlines with commercial breaks of romance and manipulation.

And you? You're not even on payroll, but you've got a starring role. You're the emotional stunt double. The supporting actor who makes their story work. You deliver the lines. You clean up the mess. You keep the show going.

But baby... **this ain't your movie.**

HOW YOU GOT CAST

It usually starts subtly:

- You feel bad for them.

- You see the good in them.

- You want to help them heal.

And suddenly, you're **managing their feelings, defending their reputation**, and **apologizing for things you didn't even do**.

Congratulations—you've been cast as "The Fool With a Savior Complex." And the worst part? The audience doesn't even know the script changed.

WHAT THE CIRCUS LOOKS LIKE

- 🎪 **You're explaining the same behavior over and over.**

- 🎪 **They create messes, and you clean them up—with your peace.**

- 🎪 **You keep believing this time will be different.**

-  **They keep you hooked with highs that never last.**

-  **You're constantly on emotional tightropes.**

And just when you try to leave? They hit you with the **love-bomb, the apology monologue, or the silent treatment soliloquy**.

You're not in a relationship. You're in a soap opera—and the ratings are tanking.

BREAKING THE ROLE: EXIT THE STAGE WITH GRACE AND GRIT

You don't need a dramatic final scene. You don't need to burn the tent down.

You just need to do one simple thing: **Stop performing.**

Stop explaining.

Stop justifying.

Stop jumping through hoops.

Let the circus collapse without you.

RECLAIMING YOUR PEACE IS THE PLOT TWIST THEY DIDN'T SEE COMING

You've been *over-functioning* for so long that silence feels like abandonment. But it's not.

It's healing.

It's choosing yourself.

It's taking your name off a production you didn't write, direct, or benefit from.

Co-Starring in Their Circus: The Breakdown

What They Do	What You've Been Doing	What You're About to Do
Start drama	Mediate and over-explain	Set a boundary
Make you feel guilty for peace	Apologize for having needs	Choose discomfort over chaos
Play the victim	Play the savior	Exit the production
Rewrite history	Doubt your memory	Believe your first instincts

A.R.K. APPLICATION:

- **Acknowledgment**: Have you been pretending their circus is just "a rough season"?

- **Respect**: Are you respecting your own boundaries—or just avoiding conflict?

- **Known**: Do they know the *real you*, or just the version that enables them?

REFLECTION QUESTIONS

- What role have you been playing in someone else's chaos?

- Are you addicted to fixing, or are you ready to free yourself?

- If peace had a voice in your relationship, what would it say?

FINAL WORD

You don't owe anyone your sanity just because you once loved them.

You don't have to be the strong one, the fixer, or the one who always "understands."

You can choose peace without a press release.

You can walk away from the circus without explaining your absence.

Let them juggle.

Let them monologue.

Let them do acrobatics for attention.

But you?

You're exiting stage left—with your dignity, your peace, and your boundaries intact.

Because this time, you're not the fool. You're the one who finally walked away.

PART IV
FREEDOM FROM FOOLISHNESS

13

RECOVERING FROM STUPID

DETOXING FROM DYSFUNCTION

"Healing begins the moment you stop romanticizing your own suffering."

— THE FUTURE YOU, SIPPING TEA AND MINDING HER BOUNDARIES

CONGRATULATIONS. YOU LEFT. NOW WHAT?

Leaving a toxic relationship is hard.

But staying gone? **That's the work.**

Because the body can walk out of the house long before the mind moves on.

You'll find yourself still checking their social media, replaying old arguments, scrolling through text threads like it's historical data.

You're free—but still detoxing.

Still unlearning.

Still grieving the version of you that clung to chaos because it felt like connection.

DETOX ISN'T PRETTY—BUT IT'S NECESSARY

Detox feels like:

- Missing someone who made you miserable.

- Crying over someone you *know* was wrong for you.

- Fighting the urge to text them *just to see*.

- Wondering if you made it all up.

You didn't.

You just got used to dysfunction being dressed up as devotion.

SYMPTOMS OF STUPID WITHDRAWAL

1. Craving the Crazy

You're tempted to reach out, not because they've changed—but because *you're lonely*. That's normal. But don't mistake loneliness for longing. That's just the echo of an empty habit.

2. Selective Memory Syndrome

You start remembering the sweet moments and forgetting the nights you cried yourself to sleep. Be careful—your brain is romanticizing survival.

3. Healing Guilt

You feel bad for feeling better. You wonder if you overreacted. You didn't. You just finally chose *you*.

HOW TO START THE RECOVERY PROCESS

Detox Step 1: Tell the Truth. The Whole Truth.

Write it down. All of it. Not just the good parts. Not just the Instagram memories. The lies. The gaslighting. The erosion of your joy. *Tell the whole story*—so you don't rewrite it later.

Detox Step 2: Block and Bless

No contact is a form of clarity. You're not being petty—you're being protective. Of your peace. Of your progress. Of your sanity.

Detox Step 3: Rebuild Your Identity Without Them in It

Who were you before them? Who are you now? What dreams did you defer because of their drama?

Your healing is the revival of *you*.

Detoxing From Dysfunction: The Breakdown

Old Pattern	New Practice
Over-explaining	Saying "No" without apology
Checking their socials	Checking in with your therapist
Wondering what they're doing	Creating what you need for you
Filling the silence with them	Sitting in stillness with yourself
Fixating on "closure"	Realizing closure is a *choice*

A.R.K. APPLICATION:

- **Acknowledgment**: What part of you is still tethered to the story?

- **Respect**: Are you respecting your journey by not returning to the scene of the crime?

- **Known**: Are you getting reacquainted with who you are outside of them?

REFLECTION QUESTIONS

- What are you grieving—the person or the potential?

- What boundaries need to be in place to protect your peace during this season?

- What are you learning about yourself now that you're no longer managing their chaos?

FINAL WORD

Dysfunction doesn't leave your life quietly.

It leaves claw marks. It throws tantrums. It tries to bargain.

But you? You're choosing freedom anyway.

You're choosing wholeness over history.

Peace over potential.

Growth over guilt.

This is your detox era.

And no, it won't be easy—but baby, it will be *worth it*.

Because the greatest flex is not who you dated... it's who you didn't go back to.

14

PROTECTING YOUR PEACE LIKE IT'S BEYONCÉ TICKETS

"Your peace is premium real estate—stop letting people squat in it for free."

— *YOUR HEALED SELF, WEARING NOISE-CANCELING BOUNDARIES*

IMAGINE THIS...

You just won front-row tickets to a Beyoncé concert.

VIP access. Backstage pass. Drinks included.

Now imagine a stranger rolling up like, "Hey, let me have that."

No thank you. No credentials. No contribution.

Would you give it up?

Exactly.

So why do we do it with our peace?

PEACE AIN'T CHEAP—STOP GIVING IT AWAY

You fought hard for your clarity.

You cried for your confidence.

You detoxed from dysfunction, and now someone wants to re-enter your life with the same chaos and *less effort?*

Not today, Satan. And not tomorrow either.

BOUNDARIES ARE NOT BARRIERS. THEY'RE BRIDGES... TO SANITY

We were taught that boundaries are mean. That saying no is rude.

That cutting people off is heartless.

But boundaries don't keep people *out*—they keep you *in alignment.*

A boundary says:

- "This is what I will and won't accept."

- "This is what honors my healing."

- "This is how you love me *well*—or not at all."

HOW TO PROTECT YOUR PEACE LIKE IT'S BEYONCÉ TICKETS

1. Check Your Access List

Not everyone gets a front-row seat. Some people belong in the balcony. Others? *Outside the building.*

2. Respond Less. Reflect More.

You don't have to attend every argument you're invited to. Not everything deserves a clapback. *Sometimes silence is the most sanctified answer.*

3. Say "No" Without a Performance

No is not a rejection. It's a recognition of your worth. You don't need to explain, apologize, or soften your boundary with a smiley face.

4. Audit Your Inner Circle

Some of your stress isn't about the devil—it's about your contacts list. If they drain you, confuse you, or trigger you, *they gotta go.*

Peace Protection: The Breakdown

Peace Violation	Boundary in Action
"Can I vent for a sec?" (again)	"I don't have the space for this today."
Unannounced pop-ups	"Please text before you come."
Emotional dumping	"I care, but I can't carry this alone."
Disrespect masked as jokes	"I don't find that funny—please stop."
Guilt-tripping over saying no	"My 'no' is not an attack—it's a choice."

A.R.K. APPLICATION:

- **Acknowledgment**: Where are you leaking peace to people who haven't earned it?

- **Respect**: Are your boundaries clear—or are you waiting for them to magically get it?

- **Known**: Do the people around you know what peace means *for you*—or just what's convenient for them?

REFLECTION QUESTIONS

- What's one area where you need stronger boundaries?

- Who in your life has been getting Beyoncé-level access with basement-level behavior?

- How would your life change if you treated your peace like a luxury, not a leftover?

FINAL WORD

Your peace is not up for debate.

It's not a discount item at the emotional clearance rack.

It's a **sacred inheritance**—and not everyone gets a key.

Protect it like it's Beyoncé tickets.

Guard it like it's the last slice of grandma's pound cake.

Defend it like it's your future.

Because when peace is present?

You think clearer.

Love wiser.

Move bolder.

15

WRITING A NEW STORY

WISDOM, GRACE & THE GIFT OF DISCERNMENT

"Just because you played the fool in the last chapter doesn't mean you can't write a bestseller in the next."

— *THE FUTURE YOU, SIGNING BOOKS AND SIPPING PEACE*

YOU'RE NOT WHO YOU USED TO BE

You've cried.

You've clowned.

You've questioned your sanity.

You've justified, defended, and denied.

But look at you now.

Not healed overnight.

Not perfect.

But *aware*.

And that, my dear, is the beginning of wisdom.

DISCERNMENT: THE GLOW-UP YOU DIDN'T KNOW YOU NEEDED

Discernment is spiritual clarity with street smarts.

It's the holy ability to **see beyond the highlight reel**.

To hear what's *not* being said.

To smell manipulation before it's sprayed with cologne.

To know when to engage—and when to **exit quietly and keep your peace intact**.

Discernment says:

- "That looks good, but it's not God."

- "That's familiar, but it's not for me."

- "That's tempting, but I've done that before—and I'm good."

WHAT WISDOM SOUNDS LIKE

Wisdom is the quiet voice that whispers:

- *"Don't chase what you had to heal from."*

- *"Protecting your peace is more important than proving your point."*

- *"Love shouldn't feel like a lesson in survival."*

Wisdom isn't loud.

It doesn't always come with applause.

Sometimes it sounds like loneliness.

Sometimes it feels like missing someone who was wrong for you.

But wisdom *never* leads you back into bondage.

WRITING YOUR NEW STORY STARTS WITH ONE DECISION:

I don't have to repeat what I survived.

You are not obligated to:

- Explain your boundaries.

- Reconnect with people just because they're sorry.

- Make your healing look palatable for others.

You are allowed to change.

To evolve.

To rise.

Without warning. Without apology. Without looking back.

New Story Energy: The Breakdown

Old Narrative	New Narrative
"I always fall for the wrong ones."	"I've learned what wrong feels like—never again."
"Maybe I'm too much."	"I'm too much for the wrong ones—and just enough for me."
"I need closure."	"Closure is the lie I told myself to stall freedom."
"I should've known better."	"I know better now—and that's what matters."
"But I loved them."	"I love me more."

A.R.K. APPLICATION:

- **Acknowledgment**: Are you still living in your old chapter—or have you stepped into your new one?

- **Respect**: Are you honoring your growth even when others don't understand it?

- **Known**: Are you finally letting *you* be known—by you?

REFLECTION QUESTIONS

- What chapter are you writing now—with your choices, your peace, your boundaries?

- What version of you are you ready to retire?

- What do you now *know for sure* that you didn't before?

FINAL WORD

You've survived stupid.

You've walked through heartbreak.

You've made peace with your past—and reclaimed your power.

Now it's time to write a new story.

A story where you're not the supporting role in someone else's fantasy.

A story where wisdom walks with you, grace covers you, and discernment leads the way.

Because foolishness might've had a chapter.

But baby—**it ain't the whole book.**

So sharpen your pen.

Set your boundaries.

Hold your head high.

This is the soft season. The wise season. The "don't play with me" season.

This is your next chapter.

And you're writing it in peace, on purpose, and *with audacity*.

CONCLUSION

STUPIDITY IS IN THE EAR OF THE HEARER

"It wasn't a waste. It was a wake-up call disguised as a relationship."

— *YOU, TELLING YOUR STORY WITHOUT SHAME*

You made it.

Through the bad choices, the bold lies, the bare-minimum texts, and the silent prayers whispered into pillows soaked with hope and regret.

You made it through the clown shows, the ghosting, the gaslighting, and the gospel-sprinkled manipulation.

You made it through the churchy advice that told you to stay, submit, and suffer.

You made it through the cycle. The confusion. The circus.

And now?

Now you're wiser.

Now you're clearer.

Now you know what stupid sounds like—and you've stopped answering.

LET'S BE HONEST ONE MORE TIME

We've all played the fool.

We've all loved potential.

We've all ignored the voice of discernment because *we just wanted to be loved*.

But here's the beautiful, audacious truth:

You can make a mistake and still be worthy.

You can fall for foolishness and still rise in wisdom.

You can start over—and not owe anyone an explanation for the peace you protected.

THIS ISN'T JUST A BOOK. IT'S A PERMISSION SLIP

To leave the drama.

To reclaim your narrative.

To laugh at what once broke you—and write better endings.

Because healing doesn't always look like therapy appointments and soft music.

Sometimes it looks like you standing in the mirror saying, "Girl, never again."

Sometimes it sounds like *blocking* instead of *praying it gets better.*

Sometimes healing is a little petty, a little savage, a little gospel, and a whole lot of **clarity**.

FINAL BLESSING

May your boundaries be bold.

May your "no" be holy.

May your peace be non-negotiable.

And may your days of choosing clowns be *canceled with immediate effect.*

Because from here on out?

You don't entertain stupid.

You observe it—from a distance.

With popcorn.

And wisdom.

Don't Let Your Wisdom Go to Waste
Share the Glow-Up. Someone Needs Your Insight.

You've made it through the chapters.

You've laughed, winced, nodded, and probably whispered "whew, that's me" a few too many times.

You've survived the circus, dropped the clown, and reclaimed your peace.

Now it's time to give someone else that same breakthrough.

Leaving a review isn't just about stars—it's about **impact**.

Your voice, your story, and your take on *The Audacity of Stupid* can help another reader feel seen, validated, and maybe even saved from their next foolish detour.

We'd be honored if you'd share a few words on Amazon or wherever you picked up this book. Your review helps more than algorithms—it helps women find truth in their own timelines.

📣 **Your Story Has Power.**

And your opinion? We *absolutely* value it.

Scan the QR code to leave a review

BONUSES

THE AUDACITY OF STUPID

BOOK CLUB DISCUSSION GUIDE

GETTING STARTED

Before diving into the questions, invite your group to:

- Choose their favorite chapter title.

- Share one "stupid" decision they can laugh about now (keep it light to build trust).

- Set the tone: This space is judgment-free, tea-filled, and truth-telling.

DISCUSSION QUESTIONS

1. The Audacity of Who?

- Which chapter hit you the hardest, and why?

- Did you see yourself more as the "fool" or the one tolerating the fool?

- How do you define "stupid" in relationships after reading this book?

2. Biblical Wisdom, Modern Mess

- In Chapter 1, we met Abigail and Jezebel. Which one are you more like in conflict—and which one are you trying to become?

- What did the stories of Adam, Job, Samson, or David teach you about personal responsibility in relationships?

3. The Mirror Moment

- What patterns did this book help you recognize in your own choices?

- Is there a past relationship or situation you now see more clearly?

- What's something you used to excuse that you now see as a red flag?

4. Political & Cultural Stupid

- How did Chapter 7 challenge your perspective on voting, politics, or identity loyalty?

- Have you ever voted (or stayed silent) in a way that didn't serve your best interests? What did you learn?

5. Trauma, Triggers, and That Inner Child

- Chapter 11 talks about your inner child loving clowns. What old wound do you think has influenced your romantic or friendship choices?

- How are you starting to reparent your younger self?

6. The Art of Walking Away

- Which chapter gave you the language or permission to set a boundary?

- Has someone ever made you feel guilty for choosing peace? How did you respond?

- How did this book challenge what you were taught about "staying strong" in relationships?

7. Wisdom & Discernment

- What's one "fool filter" you'll be applying moving forward?

- How has your definition of love shifted after reading this?

- What advice from this book would you give your younger self?

BONUS ACTIVITIES

Red Flag Rehearsal

Each person describes a red flag using a code phrase (e.g., "He only texts after 10 PM"), and the group decides:

- Is it a dealbreaker, a conversation starter, or a circus tent?

Rewrite the Script

Rewrite a real-life "stupid moment" with the wisdom you have now. Share how the story *could* have gone differently—with boundaries, clarity, or Beyoncé-level peace.

The Fool-Free Affirmation

As a group, create a one-sentence affirmation that each member can use when tempted to go back to foolishness.

Examples:

- "Peace is better than being picked."

- "I am not auditioning for chaos."

- "I can love you *and* leave you."

WRAP-UP REFLECTION

- What's your biggest takeaway from *The Audacity of Stupid*?

- How will your relationships—romantic, spiritual, political, or professional—look different going forward?

- What's one way you'll protect your peace in this next chapter of your life?

THE STUPIDITY SCORECARD

BECAUSE SOMETIMES YOU GOTTA MEASURE THE MESS

Circle each statement that applies to your most recent (or most memorable) foolish situation. Tally up your score and see where you land on the *Audacity Meter*.

PART 1: THE RELATIONSHIP RECAP

○ I stayed because "they had potential."

○ I confused chaos with chemistry.

○ I prayed instead of peacing out.

○ I accepted the apology but saw no change.

○ I blamed their trauma to excuse their behavior.

○ I googled "Is this gaslighting?" more than once.

○ My friends hated them, but I said "they don't know us."

○ I broke up with them in my head before I actually did it.

○ I went back... again.

○ I knew better—but still stayed.

PART 2: THE JUSTIFICATION GYMNASTICS

○ "They're just going through something right now."

○ "We've been through too much to give up now."

○ "No one's perfect."

○ "They didn't mean it like that."

○ "They've never had love like mine."

○ "God told me to stay." (Are you sure tho?)

○ "It's just a season."

○ "The sex is just... different."

○ "They're better when it's just us."

○ "Maybe I'm asking for too much."

SCORING: ADD 1 POINT FOR EACH CIRCLE

0–4 POINTS: *Wisdom Watcher*

You've seen some stuff, but you're learning fast. Keep those boundaries tight and your eyes open.

5–9 POINTS: *Halfway Healed, Still Hovering*

You know the signs but might need a friend to confiscate your phone on weekends. You're close—don't turn back.

10–14 POINTS: *Rewatching the Circus*

You've exited the big top but still miss the popcorn. You know it's foolishness, but the pull is strong. Time to detox, not romanticize.

15–20 POINTS: *Clown to Crown Redemption Tour*

Sis. You're not just in the circus—you're the headliner. But the good news? The curtain's closing. You've read the book. You see the pattern. You can rewrite the role. Crown incoming 👑.

✍ REFLECTION:

- What was your score?

- What did you circle that made you laugh... or cringe?

- What are you doing differently now?

- What boundary are you setting this week?